ZODIAC SIGNS

SCORPIO

October 24 – November 21

Heather Kissock

AV2
www.av2books.com

Step 1
Go to **www.av2books.com**

Step 2
Enter this unique code

EANQX1HRV

Step 3
Explore your interactive eBook!

AV2 is optimized for use on any device

Your interactive eBook comes with...

Contents
Browse a live contents page to easily navigate through resources

Audio
Listen to sections of the book read aloud

Videos
Watch informative video clips

Weblinks
Gain additional information for research

Try This!
Complete activities and hands-on experiments

Key Words
Study vocabulary, and complete a matching word activity

Quizzes
Test your knowledge

Slideshows
View images and captions

... and much, much more!

ZODIAC SIGNS

SCORPIO

October 24 – November 21

Contents

Are You a Scorpio?

Do people call you mysterious? Are you loyal to a fault? If this sounds familiar, you might be a Scorpio. A Scorpio is someone who was born between October 24 and November 21.

Scorpio is a sign in the zodiac. This is a series of 12 **constellations** that run across the night sky. For centuries, people have used these groups of stars to tell the future. The study of the stars in this manner is called astrology.

Zodiac Chart

A person's zodiac sign is determined by his or her date of birth. Which sign matches your birthday?

It's in the Stars

The zodiac constellations form a circle around Earth. In one year, Earth makes a full **orbit** around the Sun. As it does this, the Sun appears to be in different places at set times. The zodiac constellations are found along the path the Sun appears to follow.

Long ago, people used the Sun to tell the time of year. In late October, the Sun passed through the Scorpius constellation. People born then were said to be born under the sign of Scorpio.

Over time, the position of the constellations shifted. Even though the Sun now passes through Scorpio at a different time, the dates associated with the sign of Scorpio remain the same.

The main **Scorpius constellation** is made up of **18 stars**.

Antares is the largest star in Scorpius. It is **9,000 times brighter** than the Sun.

Scorpius is one of the few constellations to actually look like its namesake. The curve on the J-shaped star pattern is said to resemble a scorpion's tail.

The Myth of Scorpio

The ancient Greeks had stories about how each zodiac constellation came to be in the sky. Scorpius is linked to the Greek giant, Orion.

Orion was a mighty hunter, and he knew it. To prove his great skill, he set up a challenge for himself. Orion decided to kill every animal on Earth.

This plan upset a goddess named Artemis. She was in charge of protecting the animals. Artemis did not want them to be killed on her watch. The goddess asked Scorpio, a giant scorpion, to kill Orion. Scorpio agreed to help. He went looking for Orion. When he found the hunter, Scorpio killed him with his stinger.

Artemis rewarded Scorpio by placing him in the night sky. He can be seen chasing Orion.

Besides being the goddess of wild animals, Artemis was also the goddess of the hunt. She is often shown with hunting dogs for this reason.

Scorpio and Fixed Signs

In astrology, some zodiac signs share certain **qualities**. These qualities show how a person acts in the world. The qualities are separated into three groups. Cardinal signs are known for coming up with ideas. Fixed signs make sure everything is in order. Mutable signs help everyone deal with change.

Scorpio is a fixed sign. People in this group are known for being stable forces. They keep things running smoothly. Scorpios are also **persistent** people. They stay focused and work hard to complete projects.

Scorpios do not mind studying on their own. It allows them to concentrate on their work without distractions.

Zodiac Signs
by Quality

Cardinal Signs
Come up with ideas.

Aries | Cancer | Libra | Capricorn

Fixed Signs
Make sure everything is in order.

Taurus | Leo | Scorpio | Aquarius

Mutable Signs
Help everyone deal with change.

Gemini | Virgo | Sagittarius | Pisces

Scorpio as a Water Sign

Zodiac signs are also grouped according to the four **classical elements**. These are fire, earth, water, and air. Signs that belong to the same group share common personality traits.

Scorpio is a water sign. People born under water signs are in tune with their feelings. They use their **instincts** to deal with the world around them. Water people are considered caring and sensitive. They can also be dramatic.

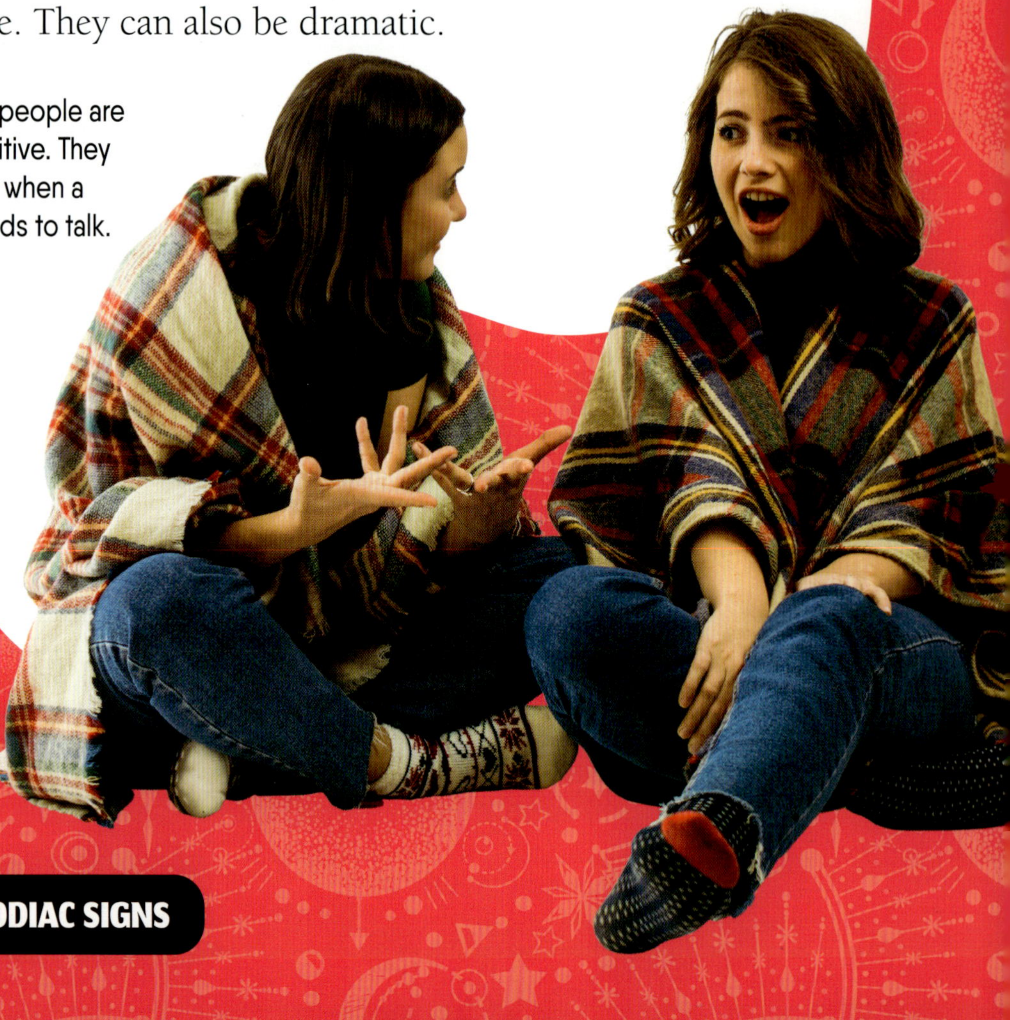

✷ Water people are highly intuitive. They can sense when a friend needs to talk.

Zodiac Signs
by Element

Being a Scorpio

A Scorpio's water traits and fixed qualities combine to create a specific type of person. A key Scorpio strength is their passion. Scorpios care deeply and have strong beliefs. They are not afraid to take action when something goes wrong.

Scorpios have their weaknesses as well. They can be jealous people. They may also seek revenge on those who have wronged them. Scorpios like to keep secrets. They may do things without telling anyone.

In **2015**, **Scorpios were the leaders of 22 countries** around the world. This was more than any other sign.

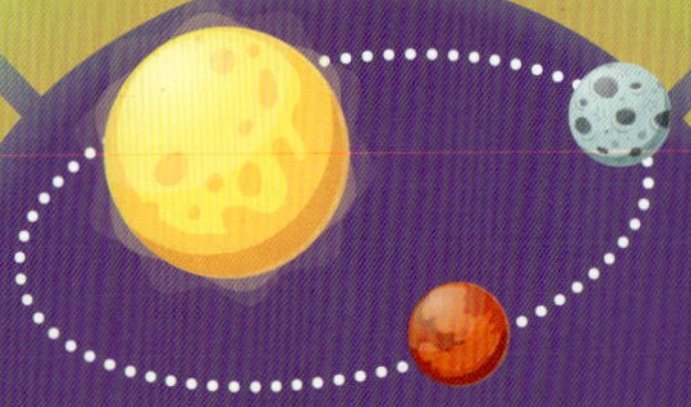

Scorpios are ruled by two planets—**Mars** and the dwarf planet, **Pluto**.

Scorpios are willing to invest their time in causes they believe in. Some show their commitment by volunteering.

Scorpios through Time

Scorpios have had a significant impact on the world over time. They have invented games, painted **masterpieces**, and discovered new planets. Their contributions have helped make the world what it is today.

Astronomer **Edmund Halley** (born November 8, 1656) observes the comet that will eventually be named after him.

1665

Artist **Jan Vermeer** (born October 31, 1632) paints *Girl with a Pearl Earring*, now on display at the Mauritshuis, in The Hague, Netherlands.

1682

1781

Astronomer **William Herschel** (born November 15, 1738) discovers the planet Uranus.

1891

University professor **James Naismith** (born November 6, 1861) invents the sport of basketball.

1903

Scientist **Marie Curie** (born November 7, 1867) becomes the first woman to win the Nobel Prize in Physics for her work on radioactivity.

2020

Actor **Joaquin Phoenix** (born October 28, 1974) wins the Academy Award for best actor for his leading role in *Joker*.

Making Friends

Some people believe that zodiac signs can help people form relationships. Each sign has its own traits. These traits can be a good fit with other signs. A Scorpio may be able to tell who would be a good friend just by knowing a person's sign.

It's Friendship

Taurus

Libra

Gemini

Scorpios get along well with people born under these signs.

It's Love

Scorpios often find romance with these signs.

Cancer

Pisces

Capricorn

It's Complicated

Scorpios find it difficult to form bonds with these signs.

Sagittarius

Aries

Aquarius

Know Your Scorpios

Scorpios continue to make an impact on the world. They can be found doing good work in various fields. Did you know these people are Scorpios?

Drake

Born: October 24, 1986

Drake started his career in entertainment as an actor on the television show, *Degrassi: The Next Generation*. He is now one of the most successful recording artists of the 21st century, with more than 170 million records sold by the time he was 34.

Drake played Jimmy Brooks on *Degrassi: The Next Generation.*

Odell Beckham Jr.

Born: November 5, 1992

Odell Beckham Jr. was **drafted** into the National Football League (NFL) in 2014. Since then, he has broken several NFL records. These include being the fastest player to reach 250 career **receptions**, which he did in only 38 games.

SZA

Born: November 8, 1990

Born Solána Imani Rowe, this singer-songwriter released her first album in 2017 and has never looked back. Her music has been nominated for several **Grammys** and an Academy Award. In 2018, she won the 2018 Billboard Music Award for Top R&B Female Artist.

Emma Stone

Born: November 6, 1988

Emma Stone began her acting career in Arizona at the age of 11. Since then, she has gone on to star in movies such as *The Help* and *The Amazing Spider-Man*. Stone won an Academy Award in 2017 for her starring role in *La La Land*.

Bill Gates

Born: October 28, 1955

Bill Gates is the co-founder of Microsoft, a company known for its computer **software**. He is considered one of the world's wealthiest people. In 1999, he founded the Bill and Melinda Gates Foundation, which works to promote global health and other issues.

The Scorpio QUIZ

1 How many constellations make up the zodiac?

2 Which Greek giant is closely linked to the Scorpius constellation?

3 What is the brightest star in Scorpius?

4 To which element group do Scorpios belong?

5 Which planets rule Scorpio?

6 What did Scorpio James Naismith invent?

7 Which zodiac signs make good friends for Scorpios?

8 Which celebrity Scorpio won an Academy Award for her starring role in *La La Land*?

ANSWERS: 1. 12 2. Orion 3. Antares 4. Water 5. Mars and the dwarf planet Pluto 6. Basketball 7. Taurus, Gemini, and Libra 8. Emma Stone

Key Words

classical elements: materials from which all other materials were once believed to be made

constellations: groups of stars that form patterns in the sky

drafted: selected to play for a team

Grammys: short for Grammy Awards, annual awards given to recognize achievements in the music industry

instincts: behaviors that a person or animal is born with and does not have to learn

masterpieces: works done with great skill

orbit: a regular, repeating path that one object in space takes around another

persistent: having the ability to stick with something

qualities: traits that make something what it is

receptions: football plays in which a player catches a pass from another player

software: programs that direct the operation of a computer

Index

Get the best of both worlds.

AV2 bridges the gap between print and digital.

The expandable resources toolbar enables quick access to content including **videos**, **audio**, **activities**, **weblinks**, **slideshows**, **quizzes**, and **key words**.

Animated videos make static images come alive.

Resource icons on each page help readers to further **explore key concepts**.

Published by AV2
14 Penn Plaza 9th Floor
New York, NY 10122
Website: www.av2books.com

Library of Congress Control Number: 2020938526

ISBN 978-1-7911-2644-5 (hardcover)
ISBN 978-1-7911-2645-2 (softcover)
ISBN 978-1-7911-2646-9 (multi-user eBook)
ISBN 978-1-7911-2647-6 (single-user eBook)

Printed in Guangzhou, China
1 2 3 4 5 6 7 8 9 0 24 23 22 21 20

062020
101119

Project Coordinator: Heather Kissock
Designer: Terry Paulhus

Every reasonable effort has been made to trace ownership and to obtain permission to reprint copyright material. The publisher would be pleased to have any errors or omissions brought to their attention so that they may be corrected in subsequent printings.

The publisher acknowledges Getty Images, iStock, Shutterstock, and Alamy as its primary image suppliers for this title.